Where Did I Come From? — Where Am I Going?

Where Did I Come From?
Where Am I Going?

Life
After Death,

the Journey of
Your Soul

Gabriele
Publishing House

The free universal Spirit is the
teaching of the love for God and neighbor
toward people, nature and animals

Where Did I Come From?
Where Am I Going?
Life After Death,
the Journey of Your Soul

Fifth Edition, POD
© Gabriele-Verlag Das Wort GmbH
Max-Braun-Str. 2, 97828 Marktheidenfeld
www.gabriele-verlag.de
www.gabriele-publishing-house.com

Original German Title:
Ich kam – woher? I gehe – wohin?
Leben nach dem Tod, die Reise deine Seele

The German edition is the work of reference for
for all questions regarding the meaning of the contents

Translation authorized by
Gabriele-Verlag Das Wort GmbH

Order No. S407TBEN
ISBN 978-3-96446-412-5

Table of Contents

Foreword

Most people are afraid of dying. We are afraid and ask ourselves, "What will happen to me afterward?"

Many say, "We don't know what will happen. No one has ever returned from the beyond." The so-called Christian churches also do not have a satisfactory answer to this existential question of life.

The question of where we come from and where we are going must seem to be a mystery to those who look at existence between birth and death as "the life."

What is explained in this book is no mystery, but the truth that many no longer know. Death does not mean cutting off our path through life, but is the gateway to its continuation on a different level of existence. It is the gateway to a life that will be more light-filled, the more consciously a person has mastered the tasks of his life on Earth.

Death — a station on the journey of our soul to the true life.

Once we understand what life really is, death loses its dread. The reality of our life continues. We, ourselves, determine "how."

The basic truths of life are revealed to us today directly from the Kingdom of God in all details through the teaching prophetess of God in our time, Gabriele.

The knowledge from the divine source contained in this book was conveyed in a series of lectures and seminars on the subject, "Life after Death — The Journey of Your Soul," in the words of the respective speakers. The content of these lectures is briefly summarized here.

Detailed explanations by Gabriele herself about the demise of the human being and the continuing life of the soul in the realms of the beyond can be found especially in the books that are presented in the appendix.

Gabriele Publishing House, the Word

I.

Where Did I Come From?
Where Am I Going?

Life After Death,
the Journey of Your Soul

Introduction

Is life — our life — only the span between the beginning and the end of our life on Earth, between birth and death, those two inevitable events that are accompanied by difficulties and often with pain for those concerned? Is there really nothing more to say about life other than that a child develops in the womb until it is born, that the person lives a few decades, dies, is buried and disintegrates into its material components? Is the soul merely a product of the physical body that perishes with it? Is the organism determined solely by the genetic make-up of the parents and ancestors, a body that develops and grows according to the laws of heredity?

Many people are convinced of this, on the other hand, others have more or less clear concepts about the continuing existence of a person or of a part of him, his soul. They believe that the deceased rests in a grave until his resurrection, and have thus carved on the gravestones: "Rest in Peace."

They think that the material body can resurrect — despite its obvious disintegration.

Those who ask the Christian institutions about life and death have to conclude that the churches are unable to make conclusive statements about what comes after death, since the Bible does not contain concrete statements on this subject. Many people who are committed to the church fear that after death they might suffer in hell or that they will be cast into eternal damnation after the so-called "Last Judgment."

The modern, enlightened person of the 21st century prefers to avoid the subject of "death." He believes that only what he can experience with his five senses and grasp with his intellect is real and exists. He recognizes himself solely in his physical existence and experiences that he is interwoven in the externally perceivable courses of life. The questions as to where he came from, where he will go and the "why" and "how come" of his fate remains enigmatic to him. Only what he experiences externally seems to him concretely tangible as his life. Due to this consciousness, which is characterized by the material point of view, he understandably shies away from contemplating an end of this existence, because he thinks that death would extinguish his existence. Thus, the human being loves this life on Earth, which, apart from its adversities, also has a number of pleasant and attractive things to offer him. He wants a long life and does not want to see others die.

For a long time, fear and ignorance placed a taboo on dying and death. This attitude has changed only gradually, after some doctors and nurses made it their task to accompany the dying and not to "shunt" them when further medical effort seems futile.

Experiences at the threshold of death have given cause for reflection and to revise one's thinking. They have encouraged people to broaden a horizon of knowledge that has become narrow concerning life. A great number of people sense or already believe in the truth of those views of life held by people in countries where the influence of materialism is less, where people see death as a station along the way in a totally natural order of life. These people are convinced that the "deceased" — that is, the soul — goes on living after the death of its physical body. It is also widely known that the soul can go through several lives on Earth in different human bodies at different times.

Even in the so-called "Christian western world," many know about the continued existence of the soul. When today, the scientists researching death publish their observations, we read some things that are by no means new; for scientific theories and ecclesiastical dogmas could displace ancient knowledge from the awareness of many people, but by no means refute or even negate the spiritual principles by denial.

What is presented in this book follows the basic experiences of humankind, but corrects many things and goes far beyond what has been known until now and into the world beyond matter, into the world of the Spirit. The knowledge that is analogously passed on here comes from there, from the Spirit of God.

*Death Is Not Destruction,
but Transformation*

"Vita mutatur, non tollitur."
Life is not destroyed, but transformed (*old grave epitaph*).

Everything is energy and nothing can be lost from this energy.

Life is energy. Just as the scientists have not yet been able to clearly define where energy comes from and why and how it develops, they cannot explain life either — but merely describe it. This energy, life, is beyond the scope of science, just as our soul is.

The soul is an essential part of the living being, "the human being." Where was it before the human being was born? Where does it go after physical death, when life disappears from the human body and this dissolves again into its components? What happens then to the "life"; what happens to the soul?

Despite the greatest scientific efforts, a research that is oriented solely to matter cannot explain what we accept as self-evident: the life, which surrounds us millionfold, for example, in the form of animals, plants and microbes. A caterpillar emerges from the egg of a butterfly; later, this caterpillar envelops itself in a cocoon; it pupates and a new butterfly slips out of the cocoon. Life changes, but it is not lost.

From the revelations of the Spirit of God, which have been given to humankind for nearly five decades, we learn that everything is energy. Life is energy — it cannot be destroyed or exterminated; only its form can change. Life in its original form is spiritual; indeed, life is spirit. Our soul is spiritual existence, a spiritual form of life.

For many people outside our Western civilization, it is part of their basic knowledge that the soul has existed before the procreation of a person and that it will continue living after his death. According to this, we are already there before our birth, in the shape of our soul, which resides as a spiritual body in the spiritual realm.

Our soul has been on a journey for a long time. Once it was a pure spiritual being in the eternal Being, in the Kingdom of God. It journeys back there, home to the eternal Father in the heavenly realms of light. Its journey leads through the soul realms, the purification planes. Under certain conditions, it "slips" into a human body, so that in a life on Earth in time and space, it discards a part of its burdens. If it succeeds in this, it can continue its journey home to more light-filled worlds of the purification planes. It has then progressed on its path.

Therefore, life on Earth is merely an intermediate station on the journey of the soul, on which the purpose is to again attain its original purity, its original light-power, its original high vibration, through a life in the law of God, the love for God and neighbor.

The soul, the spiritual formation with certain very specific "personal," as it were, characteristics, connects with the physical human body at the birth of the child. It remains connected to the body until its physical death.

The divine energy of life flows into the physical body by way of the soul and gives it life.

Everything is energy, including our feelings, thoughts, words and actions. The soul is the "book of life," in which everything is recorded that you once felt, sensed, thought, spoke and did, all of which remains active in the soul after discarding its physical body.

This means that what we take with us into the spheres beyond our identity is our consciousness, our faults and weaknesses, but also our inner joy and our orientation to God. Negative things burden our soul, shadow and darken it. Positive, selfless thoughts and actions, on the other hand, relieve the soul and cause it to be more light-filled.

Our most important task should be to be able to draw a positive balance at the end of our life on Earth, that is, to have a soul that has been relieved of several burdens and shadows. What we take with us from this life is decisive in terms of how dark or how light-filled our soul is when we die, because this determines the further journey of our soul after our physical death.

How Does Dying Take Place?
What Does the Soul Experience
When It Leaves Its Body?

For every human being, the separation of the soul from the body comes at the end of his life on Earth. However, there is no norm for "dying"; every person dies in a different way.

Modern research on dying takes its knowledge from reports of people who were clinically dead and were brought back to life. These people often suffered a more or less sudden, violent death, which, however, proved to not be final.

The reports are similar: The first experience is often a sense of floating outside and above the physical body. In this state, the soul perceives its environment and all occurrences in minute detail, for example, in the operating room or at the scene of the accident. Afterward, the soul often experiences gliding through a dark tunnel or toward a point of light. Many a one experiences being in bright light and perceives sounds, harmonies or a kind of celestial music. However, these souls are not yet completely separated from their bodies, so that attempts at resuscitation are successful.

But the natural process of dying happens in a totally different way. In this process, the withdrawal of life takes place over years. From time to time, circulatory disturbances appear; the one or the other organ may not function as before, and the body grows weaker and weaker.

During this time, many opportunities are offered to the soul to prepare for the separation from its body. For instance, while the body is in deep sleep, the soul can step out and practice "freedom of motion" with its guardian spirit. Just as someone who has been bedridden for some time has to learn how to walk again, in the same way, the soul must learn again how to move in the spiritual spheres.

Finally, the person lies down to die. Just before his soul withdraws, his whole life passes before his eyes, like a time-lapse film. Fully conscious, the soul evaluates its past, its life on Earth that has just run out, down to the most insignificant feeling. It evaluates it from a different point of view than the person did before. The determining criterion used here is that of actualized, selfless love. In this way, the soul itself becomes the "judge" over the thoughts and actions of its own person.

If the person has prepared for his death, his soul can separate from his body quite easily. Spiritual beings help the soul — its guardian spirit and the higher-developed souls of former friends and relatives. They welcome the soul that is parting from matter and help it find its place in the beyond.

However, if the person did not prepare for death, if he lived solely on the material level, without spiritual aspirations, without being oriented to God — then his thinking and striving, his whole consciousness, is so strongly fixed on the living conditions of the human life on Earth that he desperately holds on to them. He cannot imagine a life other than material, human existence and struggles against death.

Spiritual beings want to help this soul, too, so that it can detach more easily from its body. But as long as the person does not want to accept his death, or acknowledge it, their ability to help is limited, for the pure spirit beings respect free will.

The soul, which is so strongly oriented to this life on Earth, remains more or less connected with the physical body through energy currents even after it has left it. It virtually clings to its physical "house," since it thinks that life is possible solely in a material body. Under certain circumstances, it still feels what happens to the deceased body, regardless of whether it is carried to the grave or taken to the crematory.

The Soul Detaches Itself According to Its State of Development

As the human being has lived, as he has aligned his soul, in the same way the soul goes on feeling and living.

What happens to a soul, for example, during a fatal accident? If the soul is flung out of its body by a violent impact, it cannot detach itself from its body lawfully. This means that, even after disembodiment, it is still more or less strongly connected with its physical body, depending on the spiritual alignment of the person.

With such a violent separation, it is seldom possible for the soul to immediately find its way around, although its guardian spirit or other spirit beings endeavor to help. Because of the shock that the soul has suffered, it believes it is still in the body, since it still feels the momentary dread and pain long afterward, not having developed the ability to discern the difference.

The physician may have already long since pronounced physical death, the dead body may already be buried, but the soul still believes that it is connected to its body. Because of this shock, the soul may possibly be under the impression, not only for days, but for weeks or months or even longer, that it is still a human being, maybe sick or injured in an accident, but not dead.

It goes on living in these impressions, which it feels as pictures. In these soul pictures, it believes it actually lives, feels, thinks, speaks and acts in the physical body. Perhaps it goes on working at its former job, because it thinks it is still a human being. It moves in traffic and uses our means of transportation. However, after leaving the body it has no sense of feeling for time and space. It often wanders over this Earth for a long time before it realizes that some things are different than what it was used to as a human being. It may go to its friends and ask itself, "Nobody takes notice of me anymore; someone else is doing my job; I'm all alone. What's the matter with me?"

Only after such a realization can the spiritual world instruct the soul. Only once it has become aware that it is a finer-material being and that its body has long been buried, can the soul awaken due to the activities of its guardian spirit, and begin its journey according to its state of consciousness: The one soul takes the advice and lets itself be guided into the purifications planes, the other may go to its grave and wait there for the so-called "resurrection of the flesh," as it was taught during its "lifetime."

As stated in the beginning, the soul stores everything that the person experiences in the course of his life, including all religious instruction. If a person was raised according to the thinking of a certain denomination and has accepted it as the truth, his soul will remain with this creed even beyond death. This is particularly the case if the religious institution was able to convince him that it alone can grant salvation and that the prerequisite for this is the acknowledgment of all its teachings. If this soul has been released from its body, it goes on living in the concept that it still belongs to its church, and still believes, for example, that it can find God only in a church building.

But God is not bound to any place, but omnipresent as the universal Spirit, even in the soul itself. As long as a soul has not grasped this, as long as it holds on to what human teachers have impressed upon it as "truth," this influence will continue to be decisive for it. Then, it will shut itself off from what the messengers of light of eternal truth want to explain to it. It will not be able to readily find its continuing path in the beyond and will perhaps strive for a new incarnation again and again.

How different it is when a person passes away who is united with God and strove during his life on Earth to live the love for God and neighbor. Here, one can speak of "going home." This person knows that his soul originally comes from God and that it receives its life force from Him. He knows that within his soul lies his eternal and immortal life. The soul, the formerly pure spirit being, is linked with its eternal Father and wants to return to Him in the eternal homeland. The person knows that this material body can be compared to a garment that can be simply taken off when it is no longer needed. Years before he goes home, his soul receives impulses that tell it: Separate gradually from your human body.

Special vibrations of light flow into the soul. It withdraws its streams of life from the physical body very gradually. Souls from higher spheres surround this person who is linked with God, and while dying, former family members and his guardian spirit are with him. The soul, which is still in the human being, feels happy because it knows that God, the Eternal, is calling it back.

While waiting for his so-called death, the person is allowed to look back once more. He reviews his life, asks for forgiveness and forgives where he needs to forgive. Perhaps he may even see beings from the fine-material realms and he senses the fullness that surrounds him. Then the physical body closes its eyes, breathes deeply a few times, and the human being once again sees spirit beings or more highly developed, light-filled souls — then he breathes out one last time and the soul has left its body. At the same moment, this fine-material, flexible form unfolds — the soul has its "steadfastness” and lives consciously and joyfully in the spiritual sphere of vibration into which it crossed over. The soul is surrounded by light. Its guardian spirit or souls from higher worlds instruct it. The soul senses melodies; these are the vibrations of the planet toward which it tends.

Each soul is guided in a different way according to its condition. It sees perhaps a street, perhaps a tunnel or perhaps a beautiful meadow. The soul that is linked with God looks back briefly, asks for support for the mourning relatives left behind, and goes on.

This soul has made progress during its life on Earth which now lies behind it. It has come a little closer to the eternal Father for whom it longs, a few steps further along the way home, back into the light.

Where Will Our Souls Be One Day?

According to the spiritual law of gravitation — like strives toward like — the soul will be attracted to the purification plane that corresponds to it, to the souls that correspond to it.

If a person was self-centered during his life, controlled by his drives and desires, if he wanted to have and possess, if he did not love selflessly, if he hated and was envious and pursued only his pleasures — these burdens became imprinted in his soul. After it leaves the physical body, the soul takes along what the person could not recognize and reduce during his life on Earth.

The soul can also continue to develop further and higher in the beyond, though not as quickly and easily as in a human body on Earth. However, if it is unable to grasp or accept its real task, in the astral spheres of the beyond it will associate with all those who have the same interests, or it will turn back toward Earth and seek out those places where it once satisfied its passions.

Souls in whom the pull to matter is particularly strong, above all, those that are "addicted," seldom find their destination toward further development in the beyond. As so-called "earthbound" souls, they return to Earth and try to influence those people who have the same vibration, since these can carry out what the souls themselves are no longer able to do.

Thus, there are millions of ignorant earthbound souls among us; they surround us everywhere because they want a share in our lives. They practically hang like clusters of grapes on those people who live solely in the material world, because these can be influenced by them, and they can "tap into" their life force.

Therefore, when we nurture negative, not good thoughts and feelings, we give these earthbound souls the possibility to influence us. These souls, which correspond to our low, sunken state of vibration, draw strength from us and endeavor to keep us in this low vibration and, if possible, pull us down even further.

If a person has already oriented his soul to higher regions, his soul will be attracted by higher worlds after its disembodiment. If the soul has turned to God and the eternal Being, it can also be guided by the high powers of the Being. It will receive the instructions it needs and will gain the knowledge that allows it to progress. Its spiritual consciousness will gradually expand; the indwelling divine powers in it will unfold. The soul accepts the schoolings and instructions and it will continue to develop in the soul realms.

From what has been explained, we can see that if the soul has detached from its body, it will find itself again in a world that corresponds to its state of consciousness. The one who wants to know what this world will be like for him needs only to strive for self-recognition. The soul will go to that world toward which it has already oriented itself.

Thus, we merely need to ask ourselves, "Are my thoughts positive or negative? Are they marked by envy, hatred, resentment, jealousy, greed, enmity, strife? Or are they loving and selfless thoughts toward my neighbor?" From our answer, we can deduce how we are in our person and in our soul. The sphere in the beyond toward which we now tend is of the same kind.

What does the Mourning of the Bereaved Mean for the Soul?

When someone dies, he leaves behind the bereaved who mourn. The death of a person quite often means a deep, painful turning point in the life of his relatives and can give it an entirely new direction. However, the bereaved should overcome their pain and sorrow as soon as possible. For most people it is difficult to accept the death of a loved one without mourning him. Accepting this event, that is, believing in its meaning without being able to fully grasp it at the moment, is often possible only after a period of mourning.

The discarnate soul, too, feels this mourning and, with it, is detained on its further path of evolution. When mourning relatives unreasonably cling to the deceased, holding on to him wanting him back, that is, considering him their property, as it were — they bind the soul to this earthly sphere. Most people are not aware of this, nor that they are basically thinking of themselves and not of the salvation of the one they think they love so much. Such "love and sorrow" are, in truth, egotistical.

Souls have a much higher sensitivity than human beings. They suffer from the pain their relatives feel on their account.

The relatives should therefore send loving thoughts to the soul on its way home and ask God that the soul be guided further on its path of purification. In no case should the soul be held back, neither through mourning and lamentation, nor by wanting something from it.

What Is the Meaning of Our Life on Earth?

As deep as the shock over the death of a relative may be at times, we tend to quickly push the subject of death out of our consciousness, because it points to an outlook of life that we easily and often want to forget in our habitual, thoughtless, everyday life.

Every decisive experience in our life, every blow of fate give us the opportunity to reflect, to go within. Grief often leads us from a superficial "vegetating" on Earth into the depths, and touches us in areas of our soul in which the powers for a higher life lie dormant. We then perceive the impulses from the Spirit that are otherwise drowned out by our loud human activities and drives.

We should not overlook the sign from God that points out to us that we should again recognize what is essential. We should become aware that the meaning of our life on Earth is not to enjoy it to the fullest on matter.

Our life on Earth is a time of schooling and learning. We should make use of this time. If our soul does not reach the goal it is meant to learn during its life on Earth, the person will be confronted again with the same task in another life on Earth and will struggle with it until everything is resolved and expiated.

It is therefore important that we orient ourselves to the true, eternal life. It is our task to transform everything negative in our life into the positive, so that at the end, in the book of life the positive outweighs the negative or only positive things are left as a balance. Through the purification process, the soul can then become a light-filled, pure spirit being again and return to the eternal Father.

This is not possible through self-redemption, but only by acknowledging the Christ of God who, through His sacrifice on Golgotha, placed into every soul an additional power that supports us, helps us and leads us home. We call this power the Christ-spark or Redeemer-spark. But, however, when a person does not recognize his life's task and is not prepared to work on himself, to purify himself, and if he does not consciously accept Christ as his Redeemer, whose power brings about the transformation of the not good into the good — then his soul will not progress after the demise of the physical body. Instead, it will remain in the purifications planes among its own kind, according to the law "like strives to like" — or it will strive for a new incarnation.

For 2000 years, the Spirit of God has been admonishing us again and again to align with the Highest, with God, the Eternal. We should realize that the Spirit of life is in us. Each one of us knows the commandments of life, as they are contained in their essence in the Ten Commandments given through Moses. And no one can say, "I did not know anything about this!" Again and again, through the divine prophetic word, we are made aware today to pay attention to our soul, our spiritual, immortal body, to think, speak and act positively.

It is the task of our life to live — that is, to actualize and fulfill — the commandment of commandments: "Love God your Father above all, and your neighbor as yourself."

If we have lived in this spiritual alignment, then our soul can free itself after our physical death and can continue to develop itself.

For this reason, the Spirit of God admonishes each one of us: Pay attention to your soul!

The soul leaves its shell, the physical body, which dies. This process of detachment will be different for each person, but one law applies to all:

Just as a person has lived, so will his soul continue to feel and live!

Let us make an effort already now, so that our soul may become free of burdens and shadows, that it may become pure and light-filled. The divine powers in and around us will help us to draw closer to our goal, the eternal homeland of light, of peace and of love, step by step.

Questions
and
Answers

Foreword

A series of lectures on the subject of this book was held in several cities. During the discussions that followed the lectures, there was always a great interest in questions that went beyond the material presented, that supplemented it or made it more precise. They were collected and sorted, and it turned out that some questions were asked almost identically in different places.

It can be assumed that readers of this book will also have similar questions; therefore, a selection of important questions and answers is included here in Part II.

Help for the Dying Person

1.   *How should relatives and friends behave
     when a soul prepares to leave its body,
     that is, when a brother or a sister enters
     the phase of dying?*

Let us bring to mind what we would do when a loved one were to set out on a long journey. The pain of parting is present, because we will not have this person with us for a long time. We would arrange a loving farewell.

Above all, we would not leave him alone, but stay with him until he has disappeared from our view. We would help him with everything he has to arrange, settle and still put in order before his departure. We would strengthen him with positive thoughts of confidence. We would accompany him with good wishes, and we would not unnecessarily complicate the parting from the station of his life till now.

2.   What help can we give the dying person?

The dying person should not be left alone. A person should be with him who is devoted to him from the heart, who does not keep on talking to the soul and the person, but is simply there in silent prayer and loving thoughts.

We can encourage a person on the deathbed. In doing so, our help should be directed first and foremost to the soul, which is preparing to continue its journey. In the hours of dying, that is, of the passing away of the body, the soul is more awake than during its earthly life. Thus, it registers every feeling, every thought, and every word. The help we can give consists mainly in a careful enlightenment and preparation of this soul for its transition.

Here, prayer is important, because it helps to establish a connection with Christ in our inner being; and that is the prayer with the person concerned, if he wishes this and as long as this is still possible, as well as the prayer for him, that is, for his soul, that it can still forgive and thereby free itself from many a burden.

3. *What can we say and for how long can we talk directly to the soul of the dying and then deceased person?*

When the person is already unconscious, immediately before passing over, during the passing over and also shortly after. Here empathy is required, how much and what one says to him. Depending on the consciousness of the deceased, one can perhaps just briefly explain to him or his soul about the process of dying, about the detachment of the soul from the body, and then draw his attention to his guardian angel, which wants to lead the soul farther. Beyond that, what we say to the soul also depends on the relationship we have with the person who is passing on, whether we would like to give him some loving words to take with him; perhaps it is also befitting to forgive and ask for forgiveness. In any case, however, as stated, we should not talk insistently to the soul, but entrust it to Christ in love as soon as possible.

4. *The subject of "euthanasia" is discussed now and then in the media. What does it mean for the soul when its suffering is shortened by actively inducing an earlier death, as for instance, out of pity?*

Not all the relief that we want to give the dying person is a real help for his soul. We may and should support the suffering and dying body, but should neither defer its so-called death with medicines, nor shorten its life on Earth with medicines.

Genuine, positive help for a dying person consists of preparing the person for the passing of his body and, if he wishes, accompanying him in conversation and prayer. In the case of severe pain, pain-relieving medication can help to maintain the consciousness of the person and soul for leaving the physical body. In the law of cause and effect, illness and suffering serve the purification of the soul, thus, spiritually speaking, they have their purpose and fulfill it all the more if they are accepted as a chance for self-recognition and also of expiation.

5. *Does a person who has offered such active
    help in dying to another person burden him-
    self?*

More or less, yes. It depends on the motivation and the inner attitude. Basically, the following
applies according to the laws of life: The one who
interferes with the course of life on Earth, no matter whether he shortens or prolongs it at any cost,
burdens himself. When I know of a spiritual law
and violate it, this weighs more heavily than when
I act out of ignorance and in good faith.

6. *If I have actively "helped" a person to die and
    recognize afterward that I have not acted
    correctly, how can the soul forgive me?*

We should not make direct contact with the
soul, but should pray to God that He may support this soul. Christ is in every soul; He is the
connection — through Him, we can ask the soul
for forgiveness.

Thus, we should ask the soul for forgiveness solely by way of the redeeming power of the Christ of God.

Medical Help

7. *Do I act correctly in terms of the Spirit when I donate blood?*

Every cell of the body bears the very specific vibration of the person to whom it belongs. It serves him as a part of the whole. It can fulfill this function only on the place where it belongs. When such cells — in this case, blood — are transferred from one person to another, vibrational dissonances are the result. When the interaction of the forces that are attuned to each other is disturbed, this will usually lead to difficulties. This should be considered when deciding for or against transfusions. Therefore, from a spiritual point of view, there are good reasons to be opposed to transfusions and especially transplantations. As in everything, here the free will is also decisive.

The Spirit of God clarifies the spiritual correlation. But whether a person can recognize these correlations and follow this knowledge in an acute emergency will depend on the state of his spiritual consciousness. No one has the right to criticize or even condemn his neighbor for a decision he makes, because we should always respect the free will of others.

8. *We all have the obligation to preserve life. When a child is not capable of living and is then kept alive through medical intervention, can we say that one has acted wrongly toward this child?*

That the life of such a child is preserved can be founded on the possibility of a task for the soul in this incarnation. The preservation of the earthly life at any price and with all means, however, is not in the spirit of the eternal law. If a child dies prematurely, we should know that a "child soul" can develop faster in the infant and then in the realms of the beyond.

Concerning the statement, "We all have the obligation to preserve life," we can ask, in turn: Which life do we human beings mean with this? Our true life is the spiritual, the eternal life, not the one related only to the momentary one on Earth.

9. *But nothing happens by chance. In this case, the physicians are instruments. Physicians have to respect life, don't they?*

Every being is informed before its incarnation about what awaits it during its life on Earth. So when a small child takes its leave after only one day on Earth, this is may very well be a gift of grace for the soul. However, when we "artificially" hold back a soul on its path, we make ourselves complicit, according to the law of sowing and reaping, for any consequences this may have for the soul's development.

When the child can be kept alive, this is possible only because this possibility is rooted in the soul. However, the physicians should know sufficiently enough about the spiritual laws that they intervene only when it is justifiable according to these very laws. In general, we should strive in every case to follow the laws of life of the Eternal All-One and make them the guideline for our actions. The high forces that are effective in the will of God always lead us to our salvation, whether we recognize it at the moment or not.

When the Soul Leaves Its Body

10. *What happens when the soul leaves the body while the person is still alive?*

The soul can leave its body mainly while in deep sleep or unconscious, but it is still connected to the body by the so-called silver cord (like an endless, extensible umbilical cord).

According to its consciousness, the soul stays in corresponding spiritual realms and may bring back spiritual teachings from the beyond – as we know from people who were revived, that is, who were brought back to life.

The soul of a dying person can also leave the body from time to time. With a glance into the heavenly speres, it can be much easier for a soul that is about to discard its body to let go of the physical body.

11. *What does the soul look like after it has left its body?*

It resembles its former physical body. It then refines and rejuvenates itself according to its spiritual development.

12. *Most people are afraid of this transition, that is, they are afraid of dying ...*

The process of dying is similar to that of birth. To be born into a material life is a very natural event for us human beings. For the soul, it is the transition to the material plane. In comparison, to die is to be born into the spiritual worlds.

While on Earth as a human being, the very best preparation for our transition into the finer-material form of existence is to align with the light-filled spiritual realms. This takes place by turning to the Spirit of the inner being, to God, our eternal Father, and through a life in accordance with His commandment of love for God and neighbor. Those people who face the end of their present life on Earth prepared in this way will no longer be afraid, but will have hope and confidence in their alignment with Christ.

13. How can a person have hope and confidence when he learns about his path only shortly before the death of his body, that is, when it is only then that he recognizes which path he should have taken?

Every insight immediately opens a path on which we can follow this insight. The guidance through the Spirit of God, through the power of the Christ of God, is assured to us at all times, if we are willing to accept it. Enlightenment, advice and help from the Spirit of God are always available to every soul, on this side of life as well as on the other. We may safely place our hope and confidence in this.

If there is a burden in the soul that can be recognized and reduced only if the human being lives "in the world" for some time, then these experiences are simply necessary for the development of his soul, so that he can be brought to see reason and be led further. He can then often cover a good distance on the path to God while still in this life on Earth.

14. *A person has died and was declared clinically dead. He actually experienced dying. He
knows that he died; it was his last thought.
But he is brought back to life. Does the same
soul enter the body of this person again?*

Certainly, because in this case, the separation
of the soul from the body has not yet taken place;
otherwise, the soul could not be brought back at
all — the silver cord still connects body and soul.

15. *In an accidental death, the soul is suddenly
flung out of its body. Does the soul have difficulties adjusting after such a sudden disembodiment?*

When a soul is suddenly flung out of the body,
this usually means a shock for the soul. But we must
make a difference here as well: Is it a person who
has begun to align with God, or is it a spiritually
unknowing, possibly only materialistically oriented
person?

Decisive for the condition of the soul after its disembodiment is in each case the consciousness that it developed during this school on Earth. The shadowed soul takes the consciousness of its former human being with it into the beyond — its consciousness does not reach beyond the earthly, material world. The spiritual beings coming to its help are either not recognized or are even rejected. So it can take a long time until this soul understands and accepts its new situation.

In contrast, a spiritually oriented soul accepts gratefully the help offered by the spiritual world and is also able to find its way into the purification planes corresponding to it without too much difficulty.

16. *What about the souls of those who are murdered or were sentenced to death?*

The person sentenced to death knows that he will die. He will prepare himself according to his consciousness and will experience on the other side what corresponds to the vibration of his soul.

It could very well be that the person who is suddenly murdered has a similar experience to that of the victim of an accident.

However the process of dying takes place — in the hereafter, what awaits each soul is what corresponds in each case to its consciousness. Each soul is instructed; it is given the possibility to recognize its burdens and is shown the way of clearing things up. Whether it accepts the teachings is in the free will of each soul.

17. *When the soul discards the body, does it then see the Godhead?*

Here, too, the state of consciousness of the soul is decisive. If the soul is fully purified at that moment, it will not be long before it achieves the vision of God. But most of us have to take our way through the purification planes for quite some time before we can step before God as light-filled souls.

Burial of the Body
Contact with the Deceased

18. *Does cremation damage the soul? May one
    burn a corpse?*

This again depends on the state of spiritual
development of each individual. The one who has
made use of his life on Earth can release his soul
from his body more quickly.

As long as a person is still very earthbound,
the soul will feel pain when the body is burned,
because it is still more or less connected with its
former body.

19. *May we think of the deceased, or do we pull
    them back to Earth with this?*

It depends on the content of the thoughts.
Thoughts are energies that can bind. The best we
can do for those who have left this Earth before

us is to lovingly release them into their new life. As soon as it is possible for us, we should stop thinking of them as still being a part of our life on Earth.

Selfless prayers for our deceased are the most beautiful service of love we can give them.

20. *Isn't it quite natural that I think of my departed child or husband? Shouldn't I honor their memory?*

Surely this is understandable especially in the initial period after the passing of loved ones. But we certainly want the best for them, and therefore, as stated, we should lovingly release their soul into their new life.

It can also be helpful to us to become aware of who "my husband" and "my child" are. Neither one of them is our possession. They are independent spirit beings, souls, which have walked a part of their path at our side during this earthly journey, so that we clear up with one another and release what binds, or has bound, us to one another in the law of sowing and reaping. We should also act toward them according to the commandment of love, which we are commanded to do for all our neighbors. Once the common journey is finished, that is, once they depart from this earthly life, we may not hold them back. To let them go on freely, to not bind them to us by unreasonable claims of ownership, that is true, selfless love. "To honor their memory" — this is not diminished by doing so.

21. How do the bereaved who are mourning detain a deceased person's soul on Earth?

On the one hand, by an utterly selfish request of the bereaved, such as, "Stay here! Don't leave us! Help us!" Usually, the soul cannot resist such requests. And on the other hand, through the binding, which is not dissolved by death — for example, dependencies, unforgiven things, unatoned things, reproaches and the like.

Let us also remember that mourning can easily turn into self-pity.

22. *Should one keep on going to the cemetery for years to visit the grave of a deceased person, or does this bind the soul to oneself?*

If the soul has recognized the truth and thus its spiritual path, it does not let itself be detained by this. This again depends upon the state of consciousness of the soul.

Visiting graves can also be done out of tradition or self-pity on the part of the mourner, and can perpetuate, both in the bereaved person and in a soul still inclined to toward the Earth, a binding that actually should be dissolved.

23. *Can we ask a deceased person for forgiveness?*

Yes, but we should not address the deceased directly, because we then pull his soul back to

Earth. We should ask the deceased for forgiveness through Christ.

24. *I have heard that we will see each other again as souls in the heavenly spheres ...*

Every soul can ascend only as far as it has developed. Thus, whether we will come together in the realms of the beyond is a question of similar vibrations.

Once we have completed our path of purification, we will reunite with all our loved ones as spirit beings in the eternal homeland.

25. *What do you think about geneological research?*

Genealogical research is not in the law of God, because the researcher binds himself to the past by "digging up the dead," so to speak, thus possibly bringing them back and binding them to himself again. By so doing, he as well as the souls of his ancestors, are delayed in their further evolution. And if there are still earthbound souls among them, we thus give them the opportunity to cling to us, so as to accomplish through us what they have not yet let go of.

The helping messengers of God unceasingly endeavor to help each and every soul; all high powers of light are at their disposal for this. Those spirit beings that have been entrusted with the protection, teaching and guidance of the soul, serve the soul out of the power of divine love and wisdom and will do everything possible to bring their charge to where it will be happier. Their activity is limited solely by the free will of the soul, which can accept or reject their help.

However, what we can do for the souls of our ancestors is to pray for them. Through prayer, one can help, and this is lawful.

26. *What can one do when a soul, despite our prayers, contacts us again and again?*

Here we can first ask ourselves, with what thoughts or feelings are we possibly holding back the soul – and then clear that up! Let us also continue to pray, however, not to the soul, but to Christ. We ask Him to help the soul to detach itself and continue on its path. There is a strong power in selfless prayer.

As a result of our own spiritual higher development, it is possible for us to be freed from the intrusiveness of a soul – a bound soul can come to reflection by experiencing how a person escapes its influence through a higher spiritual development. Through this, the soul may gain insight and will, in turn, take the path to the light.

*27. How can we help a deceased person with
    prayer, if everything goes according to the law
    of cause and effect anyway?*

Everything is energy — thus, our selfless
prayer is a positive force that can benefit the soul
of a deceased person. Thereby, the effect of the
sown cause can be mitigated. To what extent the
effect is mitigated or cancelled, only the eternal
Father knows. Certain is that God, the Eternal, is
the eternal Giver in all that He brings about. He
knows best how to guide and help His children.

*28. Isn't it presumptuous to ask the eternal
    Father for something?*

We should even ask our eternal Father to give
the souls more strength so that they are able to
repent. Christ tells us again and again: "Pray for
your neighbar." As stated, positive energy can be
released through loving devotion in prayer.

29. May we also pray to the guardian spirit?

Pray to the eternal Father or to Christ. Through this, you will also reach the guardian spirit. If you want to think lovingly of the guardian spirit, that also has an effect — but always pray to the highest, namely, to the eternal Father or to Christ.

30. May one pray for a disembodied soul?

We should always pray to Christ that He give the soul strength for insight, but never directly to the soul, because there is the danger that we bind ourselves to it. Therefore, we should always commend a soul into the guidance of the Christ of God.

Suicide

31. *What happens when someone commits
    suicide?*

With a suicide the separation of the soul from the body takes place similarly as already described. However, what the person and the soul thereby feel is always different, depending on the state of consciousness and the burdening of the soul.

After disembodiment, it is also possible for the soul of a person who commited suicide to regret its deed when it looks back — no soul is lost, before God, the Eternal, brings all His children back to the eternal homeland from which we once went out.

However, it should be said about suicide that basically escape from self-created causes and their effects is not possible. The soul takes its causes along with it into the realms beyond and will have to expiate them later. It is clear that suicide burdens the soul for a long time, often through several future incarnations.

32. *Is the time of death also predetermined for the person who commits suicide?*

No, by bringing his life on Earth to a premature end, that is, by committing suicide, the person is carrying out a drastic form of unlawful human self-will, even if he does so out of despair and adversity.

33. *What consequence does suicide have for the soul concerned?*

This varies from soul to soul, depending on what is involved. Basically it can be said that the soul of a person who takes his own earthly life is not able to continue immediately, in order to ascend to the pure worlds step by step. It lives on in soul pictures with all the problems that drove it to suicide, but it no longer has the possibilities to solve these problems as formerly, in the life on Earth.

34. Can someone who committed suicide incar-
nate again?

Every soul that is still bound to the Earth by the ties of burden will want to go back to the Earth, that is, to incarnate again.

35. Everything should be better organized in the
beyond. There should be angels that guide
the souls and help them. Souls surely cannot
wander about endlessly!

There is no lack of organization or of angels, but souls that were stubborn and unteachable as human beings on Earth are the same in the beyond. This is why it is often so difficult to instruct them. Here on Earth, too, don't we do many things that we know we should not do?

But these souls do not wander about "endlessly." They are constantly offered help and at some point this help will bear fruit. The homeward-leading and homeward-striving force, the Christ-spark, lies in each burdened soul. Through this spark, each and every soul will sooner or later find its liberation.

36. *I had to watch how a healthy mother became ill with cancer. She then killed herself with tablets, because she was in despair. She didn't do anything wrong, did she?*

An illness always wants to tell something to the person affected. If a disease or illness appears in the body, it usually means that the burden of the soul wants to flow out into the material body — possibly, a whole complex of set causes is released from the soul into the body.

If we try to block soul burdens from rising up, this sets us back in our spiritual development.

We should therefore also practice turning to the Inner Physician and Healer, Christ, in thankfulness when a physical ailment strikes us and we are close to despair. In the present case, the woman could have taken pain-relieving medications for support, for example, and with the help of Christ could have recognized her soul burden and possibly cleared up many things. In the soul realm, this is not possible for her so quickly. — Perhaps even a healing would have been possible.

37. *It was just said that the woman could have taken pain-relieving medications. I always thought that the Spirit of God does not condone the use of painkillers ...?*

The commandments of God do not contain any forbiddance; everyone is free to decide. The motivation and attitude of the individual is always essential. Through pain-relieving medication, one can make the pain more bearable for old and very ill people, so that they can still align with God, the Eternal, during their last days.

38. *Is death already preprogrammed at the time
    of birth?*

Yes, but we can shorten our life through wrong behavior; with correct behavior, we can also lengthen it, under special circumstances.

39. *How can the faults a person has committed
    out of ignorance be assessed?*

The consequences are not as serious as those of the faults committed by a knowing person. If one has come to recognize himself, one can ask that the faults previously committed are forgiven. In other words, one asks the wronged person for forgiveness. If the latter is no longer in his earthly garment, one asks him for forgiveness by way of Christ. In this way, this request will surely reach its goal.

40. *If soul burdens have flowed out of a sick body
and the soul goes over into the beyond, does
the soul take along the remainder of the burdening?*

If there is anything remaining, the soul takes
it along.

41. *What is the reason for an infant's death?*

Often the soul still has to expiate only a very
small burden, which it can resolve already with the
short incarnation into a human body.

42. *Isn't it an unusual punishment to have to die
as a child or even at birth, and not come to
have a life?*

We human beings are so used to regarding our
physical life as *the* life, that it is often difficult for
us to accept what the Spirit of God wants to make
us aware of: Our true, original, imperishable life

is our spiritual existence. This spiritual existence was there before our incarnation and will continue to exist afterward.

The soul of the child, which leaves the earthly body again after a very short stay in the temporal, therefore does not lose its life, but rather continues on its way back to the eternal homeland; thereby, it is accompanied by spiritual beings in the beyond. This knowledge helps parents and relatives to more easily overcome the shock of the child's unexpected passing.

It is possible that an incarnation as such is already the expiation of burdens. Since the child has no time to burden itself anew, a part of or even the rest of the burdening that the soul had previously borne is taken away in this short incarnation of the soul.

43. *Do our bodies resemble one another from one incarnation to the other?*

Yes.

44. With which souls do we come together again?

This is a question of similar vibration and burdening. Like always draws to like.

45. When does the soul lose its reminiscences?

The soul remembers its past lives in the spiritual planes; when it goes into a new incarnation, the memory is covered up. We human beings should not strive for knowledge of our past lives. What we are to recognize now, in order to work our way up to a higher consciousness, is shown to us in this life on Earth each time with the energy of the day.

46. We know that we have all been on Earth several times already. When my soul now leaves my body, do I then know about my previous lives, everything I have done?

Yes, we then know about our previous life.

47. *And if I have then not developed myself any further?*

If we have not used our life on Earth to develop the love for God and neighbor, then we have not fulfilled the purpose, the task, of this incarnation; this means we have not used the divine energy and strength; it is possible that we have burdened ourselves even more.

We can also see it this way: When we do not attain the goal of a school grade here on Earth, we have to repeat that grade before we can go on to the next one.

48. *Can a soul look into its former family?*

Yes, but it should not do this and a higher developed soul has no need for this.

49. *Surely my freedom also includes the overview so that I can recognize my own faults?*

Certainly, we get that, too. Before going to Earth, the soul is shown the possibilities of the incarnation ahead of it.

After laying down the body, the soul can again see everything that it was able to fulfill in the past incarnation, and also what still lies ahead.

Before it steps out of its physical body, the soul can again experience its past life as in a fast-motion film. It itself then recognizes to what extent it was able to actualize its purpose, whether it passed the "grade," whether it has drawn a bit closer to the eternal homeland.

50. *If in a previous life, a person experienced something which caused him much anguish and is now stored in his soul, when he incarnates again will he perceive a warning when something similar is about to happen, so that he can shy away from doing the same again?*

We are always warned by our conscience via inner impulses when we are in such danger. The question is whether we listen to them at all and want to follow them accordingly.

The Spirit of God does not leave us in ignorance. Today, in our time, we are offered the chance to walk the Inner Path. The more we grow in knowledge about ourselves, the more we will be aware of what is registered in our soul garments. Little by little, soul-pictures then rise up in us. In this way, we can overcome the past step by step. Thus, it is not so that we remain unknowing about what burdens us.

51. *What happens, for instance, when civilians suddenly lose their life because of war, that is, without a recognizable guilt? I do know that the cause is karmic, but perhaps this can be explained again.*

From the teachings of the Spirit of God, we know: Everything is energy, and no energy is lost

— this is also known to us from science, as well as the principle: Action equals reaction. In the tradition it is said: What a person sows, that he will reap.

Every set cause comes into effect at some point, unless the person has recognized his wrong-doing in time, repented, asked for forgiveness — and obtained forgiveness — and, if possible, made amends for what he was guilty of.

Particular referring to killing, Jesus of Nazareth clearly said: *The one who takes up the sword will perish by the sword.* So when people who are not involved in an act of war themselves suffer under it or even die, it is quite possible that through belligerent thoughts and the affirmation of armed conflicts, that is, also through their active thoughts, they were involved in it or were partly responsible in a previous life on Earth for the fact that many of their fellow people died in warring events at that time. Due to the fact that they now die in an act of war, the soul receives the possibility to expiate this burden.

However, this by no means excuses the perpetrator, for by killing a human being he has violated the law of neighborly love and God's commandment: "you shall not kill," thus setting a new cause.

This is, as stated, *one* possibility in the law of sowing and reaping. Who has set what portion of a cause, and what corresponding effects are to be borne by the individual, is precisely weighed and measured according to cosmic justice.

The Purification Planes

52. *After the death of the body, time and space no longer exist for the soul. But where will the soul then be?*

This depends entirely on the state of consciousness of the individual soul, according to how the person has lived and whether the soul is still strongly earthbound or listens to the helping hints of its guardian spirit, who accompanies it in the beyond on its further journey across the purification planes.

The eternal Being is seven-dimensional and has nothing to do with our perception of time and space.

In the increasing densification through the Fall, seven Fall-realms, seven different vibrational planes, were created. However, these are not arranged successively, but flow into one another. Each planet of the various galaxies is surrounded by all seven levels. After the demise of the body, the soul goes to one of the four purification planes where it finds the vibration that corresponds to the state of its soul vibration. If it follows the purification path of the soul and is not drawn to a new incarnation, then on its further path it very gradually reaches the three preparation planes, on which it prepares itself for its return home, as a spirit being that is again pure into the eternal Being.

The soul is the book of life, which bears in itself all a person's expressions of life stored in pictures as on a film. As a soul in the purification planes, we see everything in pictures, live in them and feel in and on our soul body what the pictures convey to us, light and shadow — the good, the less good, what we have done to our neighbors and also to our fellow creatures, the animals.

Every person is different, and dying takes place differently with every person — therefore, in the beyond, every soul is also individually instructed and led farther.

How each soul behaves and whether the soul accepts the teachings lies in its free will; no soul is compelled to do anything.

54. *The Earth is the only place where all levels of consciousness exist together and at the same time. Are there other planets where fully material beings live?*

The Earth is the only place where material beings live.

55. *It is said that the Earth is the lowest point in the universe. Are the souls that dwell on Earth exclusively those that are the farthest from God, or can other souls also dwell here on Earth, with or without a body?*

The Earth is the farthest point from God in the universe and the only place where beings from all levels of development and from all levels of consciousness are found. It is inhabited by human beings whose souls have extremely distanced themselves from God, as well as by those people whose souls have a higher degree of spiritual maturity. All levels of spiritual development can be found on our planet, up to pure beings of light that have incarnated on this Earth to rescue and bring home the fallen, shadowed souls.

Among the people on Earth, many pure spirit beings perform their service as guardian angels, as they do everywhere in the Fall-realms.

Of the disembodied souls, only the earthbound, strongly shadowed ones linger in the area of the Earth.

56. *I read somewhere or other that after its physical death, the soul goes to certain spheres of the beyond, and there takes a rest and is then instructed. I cannot quite see how earthbound souls fit into this.*

We heard earlier that the situation of souls varies a great deal when they pass on. Just as the tree falls, so does it lie.

If someone is oriented only to the material and sees only the externalized life here on this Earth as "life," then his soul will want to continue to be active on Earth. It will not even seek the possibility to go farther and often will not listen to the teachings of the spirit beings.

Due to its freedom of will, it therefore remains in the Earth sphere and remains an earthbound soul — until it sees reason and allows the guiding angel to lead it farther on its way into the purification planes.

57. *Therefore not every soul will automatically see the light after its disembodiment ...*

That's correct — as stated: Just as the tree falls, so does it lie.

58. *What is the task or work of a soul after its physical death?*

To fill with light and cleanse all the soul particles that it burdened. This filling with light and clearing up takes place by recognizing its faults, repenting and awakening in itself the love for God and neighbor. This is also possible as a soul, through the selfless service of love to other souls.

59. *After the death of a person, is it possible for the soul to return in an animal?*

The incarnation of a soul into the body of an animal is not possible.

60. *A soul can continue to develop as a soul, but can it also burden itself?*

It is not possible to burden itself any further; however, it could stay in its present condition for a long time, this means that it will not progress or will progress only slowly.

61. *If a person was a strong drinker, and now its earthbound soul goes into pubs and bars and*

*clings to drinkers in order to drink with them
— doesn't it burden itself?*

Even an earthbound soul cannot burden itself
any further. It lives in a dream, so to speak, even
when, for example, it clings to drinkers and thinks
it is drinking with them. Every person, even the
drunkard, has a free will, which he does not have
to subordinate to an earthbound soul. Nor does a
person in an earthly garment burden himself when
he commits a crime, for example, in a dream.

62. *Does an earthbound soul have the freedom to
do whatever it pleases without consequences?
Can it act unlawfully without consequences
for itself?*

An earthbound soul can only influence people
who let themselves be influenced. We are exposed
to many dangers and temptations on Earth. We
have to prove ourselves constantly. We can burden
ourselves only if we give in to these influences.

63. *Where will criminals be after they die — for example, murderers or people who violate nature?*

A disembodied soul feels, thinks, wants and acts just as the person was. It behaves according to its state of consciousness and remains in its sphere of vibration.

According to the law of "like attracts like," it is surrounded by those like it: If it should be on Earth, by people who correspond to its sphere of vibration, and in the purification planes, again by like-vibrating souls. In the soul realms, a soul is surrounded almost exclusively by those that are like it; similar souls act on it like mirror images. It is also held there by a kind of group spirit. But also these souls are not without a guardian spirit, that is, they are not without further spiritual impulses, which will ultimately bring them back, step by step, to the eternal homeland. But in the soul realms, for the reasons mentioned, it is considerably more difficult for such a soul to develop further and higher than on Earth.

64. *How does the clearing of burdens and a spiritually higher development take place in the purification planes?*

The path of purification of the soul is much more difficult and time-consuming in the realms beyond than on Earth. Although the concept of time exists only in matter, it can still be said that it takes longer "over there" to purify and lighten the soul body.

In principle, here as there, a higher spiritual development is based on the development of selfless love. Here as there, the path back to God, the path of the love for God and neighbor goes by way of self-recognition and by clearing up and discarding the not-good. These processes take much longer and are sometimes considerably more painful in the soul realms than in a human garment on Earth, because the soul sees in its soul body the suffering and pain it has inflicted on others as a human being, and suffers and endures this itself on its soul body.

65. *Will the soul of a child arrive in the beyond as an adult or as a child?*

A child that has died is also a child as a soul in the beyond, and there, too, it needs to develop like it would have here on Earth — however, there in the children's sphere that corresponds to its consciousness.

The souls of children are still much more open for the teachings of the Spirit. They accept more readily the heavenly divine order and the possibilities of spiritual reality and thus develop quickly. Since they are not yet so strongly shaped and bound by an intellectual way of viewing things, they grow and mature less hindered than a soul that was imprinted by a long life on Earth. Their development in the soul realms takes place in the joy of discovering new spiritual possibilities. They still more or less grasp the totality and are still close to it. They expand their consciousness without much difficulty or effort, as at play. This is why we speak of the "children's spheres."

66. *What is the particle structure of the soul?*

The fine-material body of the pure spirit beings in the Kingdom of God is made up of a particle structure; it is an absolutely flexible structure through which the immeasurable primordial power radiates, the All-consciousness. The particles are arranged similarly to the scales of a fish; each particle is permeated by the light of the universe, the law of the Kingdom of God. The soul, like the spirit bodies of the heavenly beings is also made up of a particle structure, except that the particles of the soul are shadowed.

67. *Can it be a protection when the knowledge about one's former life on Earth is covered up during a new incarnation?*

Yes, absolutely, because if we could see all our burdens from our last life, we would not have the courage and confidence for a new beginning.

68. *If one would make efforts to let go of his faults from one day to the next, would it then be possible to gain the inner vision?*

A person who consistently discards his faults and lives a God-conscious life can attain the constant inner connection with Christ, so as to be led directly by Him.

However, discarding one's faults takes place step by step. Discarding all faults at one blow cannot succeed.

69. *Can a person manage to pass all levels in one lifetime?*

Yes.

70. *I am 80 years old; I know that my life is coming to an end. Now I would like to know: what can I still do? I have heard only just now about the Inner Path.*

It is never too late to turn to Christ in us and to orient ourselves every day to Him and His commandment of love for God and neighbor. The Ten Commandments of God and the teachings of the Sermon on the Mount of Jesus of Nazareth serve as a standard for our lives.

The Christ of God knows how to guide each one of us, whether younger or older. With His strength we can use every day of our life on Earth to live more and more in the awareness of "God in us," in order to recognize ourselves, to discard our faults and weaknesses, to forgive our neighbors and ask them for forgiveness and to make amends for what is still possible.

71. *Everything that I process intellectually can help me to understand the correlations better. Today also brought a lot that is worth knowing. To what extent does this knowledge help me on my path?*

Our knowledge is like knowing a map that points out the way for us and helps us to more quickly and better find our around in a new country. However, ultimately, all spiritual knowledge is of value only when we actualize it.

72. *Can we see it this way: When I don't feel well, then there are probably souls that are influencing me?*

When souls can influence us, it always starts with us bringing ourselves into a lower vibration — by our giving in to lower feelings and thoughts. We even let them grow in us. When we remain in this low vibration without realizing it and saying, "Stop, dear friend, where are you heading again?" — then the souls that are on this vibration approach and influence us even more. For like attracts like; this is a divine law. Thus, we also attract those souls that are bound to this level of vibration on this Earth. They can then pull us down even more if we do not put a stop to our negative feelings and thoughts.

73. Aren't there also a few good spirits here?

Of course, our guardian beings are here; and there are countless pure spirit beings that try to guide the people. Let us ask ourselves, for instance: How did we learn about this spiritual knowledge? How are people guided into a positive direction? *Nothing* happens by chance, and so, these our guardian beings direct us human beings, again and again, to where we have the opportunity to find our path. Of course, we have the freedom to accept this guidance or not.

74. Does food have an influence on the development of the soul?

Very definitely: The Spirit says very clearly that we should nourish ourselves from the fruit that the Earth gives us willingly. Of course, depending on the present level of consciousness of the individual, that will not be 100% possible right away.

The Spirit advises us to proceed step by step. When, for example, someone eats meat, he can try to reduce it slowly. One should not just do this for external reasons of health, by saying, "This meat is not good for my body," but out of the conviction that the animal is my second neighbor and that when I kill it for my nourishment, I have killed.

A harmonious spiritual development includes all spheres of life, including nourishment, because: Everything is vibration. However, this knowledge has been partly buried over the course of the centuries.

75. *Can one walk the Inner Path when one still eats meat?*

The person who wants to walk the Inner Path is not imposed upon with rules about eating.

On the Inner Path, the path of love for God and neighbor, toward people, nature and animals, we ourselves come to realize what is right. Out of love for the eternal Father and His creatures, we will be able, from within, to gradually let go of what does not correspond to the divine law.

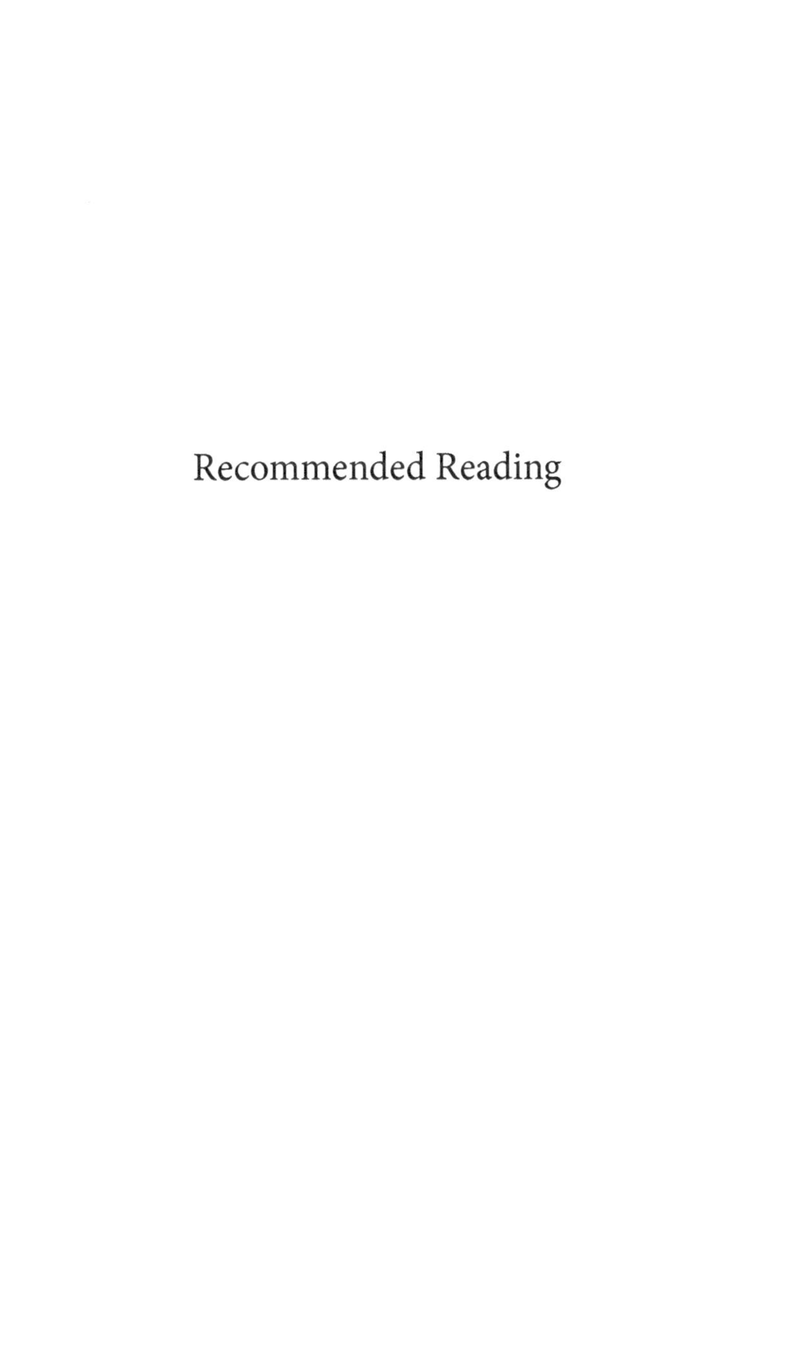

Recommended Reading

Astral Horror

It is not the words that are so terrifying, but the reality of what is described in it. For example, how "astral hackers," that is, earthbound soul from the beyond, hack into the life programs of people, how they can influence them and make them compliant, how programs of addiction have an impact in the beyond, and much more...

Gabriele points out that this side of life and the beyond are not separate and that a person's works follow him, taken along in his soul. But we all have a guardian being at our side — because God, the Eternal, fights untiringly to guide us all back to the eternal homeland.

124 pp., SB, Order No. S 340en, ISBN 978-3-89201-806-3
Also available as an E-book.

The Path of Forgetting

The Microcosm in the Macrocosm

The truth about each one of us is in the stars. How are we to understand that?

The universal correlations between the microcosm and the macrocosm are explained in such a way that they comprehensively convey the lawful processes that are behind all life. Gabriele explains that all that we feel, speak and do, all our emotions are recorded in a gigantic communication and memory system. She explains the significance of our life on Earth, as well as the possibility of reincarnating or of continuing to develop on the "path of forgetting," back into the sole reality, the true eternal homeland.

112 pp., SB, Order No. S 348en, ISBN 978-3-89201-807-0
Also available as an E-book.

The Soul on Its Path to Perfection

Gain until now unknown insights into the makeup of Creation and of the soul, as revealed by Christ through the prophetess and emissary of God, Gabriele. Christ extensively explains the path of the soul, its homeward path from the Earth into the Father's house. His word of revelation in this book gives answers to many questions, for example:

What does the soul have to recognize and learn on the individual levels?

What is it like for a soul that has left its physical body during its early years?

What is it like on the planets and the spiritual dwelling places in the soul realms? And much more.

The revelation from Christ gives knowledge about the meaning of our life on Earth as well as courage and assurance for the continuing life of our soul. God, our eternal Father, never forsakes us. Every soul is guided and taught according to its degree of maturity.

The path of the soul back into the Kingdom of God, to the eternal homeland, goes by way of seven times seven consciousness levels, from Order to Will, then Wisdom, Earnestness all the way to Patience, Love and Mercy. To activate these levels of the soul is the task of every soul here on Earth and in the spheres of the beyond.

116 pp., HB, Order No. S 209en, ISBN 978-3-89201-952-7
Also available as an E-book.

We will be happy to send you free of charge
the current catalog of our books as well as the many
free excerpts to various topics.

Gabriele Publishing House – The Word

North America: P.O. Box 2221, Deering, NH 03244
Toll-free Order No. 1-844- 576-0937

Germany: Max-Braun-Str. 02, 97828 Marktheidenfeld
International Orders: +49.(0) 9391-504-843

www.gabriele-publishing-house.com